Facing Pain — Embracing Love

"In his extraordinary new book, Jim Warner teaches us that embracing love empowers us not only to face our pain, but also to transform it into beauty, soulful connection, meaning, and joy. Jim has found the elusive spiritual link between love and pain."

—Raz Ingrasci, President and CEO, Hoffman Institute Foundation

"Life is fraught with both expected and unexpected twists, some self-induced and some imposed upon us. With wisdom and compassion, Jim Warner reveals how we can navigate the pathways of love and pain toward authentic living."

—Jim Jameson, Past Chairman, Young Presidents' Organization (YPO), and founder/major shareholder of companies in aerospace, agriculture, publishing, book distribution, and real estate

"Jim Warner makes a strong case for why accomplishment and accumulation inevitably fall short in our quest for lasting happiness, and how real fulfillment always has its roots in service and stewardship. I would recommend this book for anyone exploring deeper meaning and enjoyment in their lives."

—Rob Follows, Chair, YPO Social Enterprise Networks; Founding Partner, STS Capital Partners; and climber of Mount Everest and Seven Summits

"Jim thoroughly understands the complex lives of CEOs today. In this book, he shares invaluable guidance on balancing challenges and living a meaningful life."

—Jill Kinney, Managing Director, Clubsource, and member of YPO International Forum Board

"Great love and great suffering are the natural initiations available to all humans, inside or outside any formal religion. In fact, they are the most effective spiritual teachers of all. Jim Warner makes such patterns both clear and compelling."

—Richard Rohr, OFM, Founder, Center for Action and Contemplation, and author of *Everything Belongs* and *Quest for the Grail*

"We can't navigate our life's journey unless we know our current position. *Facing Pain—Embracing Love* shines a light on where we stand today and what we need to do to move towards a more authentic life. Using a clear, succinct writing style, Jim teaches us that more significant than reaching the final destination are the real gifts we receive along the way: the people we meet, the challenges we encounter, and the lessons we learn. A powerful, must-read for anyone ready to lift the facades and create genuine connections."

—Michael Bloch, Founding Chair, YPO Transitions Network, and private investor

"Jim Warner's work is legendary among YPO/WPO members. His new book, *Facing Pain—Embracing Love*, delivers an easy-to-understand, yet profound, life-changing message. This is what you've been seeking, though you may not realize it."

—Frank Buonanotte, CEO, Barrett Rand Corporation, and a member of YPO

Facing Pain — Embracing Love
The Map to Authentic Living

Jim Warner

OnCourse International
Boulder, Colorado

Published and distributed by
OnCourse International
2160 Meadow Avenue
Boulder, CO 80304 USA
Tel: +1 303.449.7770   Fax: +1 303.449.8497
www.oncoursein.com
Contact us for information on author interviews
or speaking engagements.

First Edition
Printed in Canada

This edition is printed on acid-free paper.

Designed by Kayla Morelli

Publisher's Cataloging-in-Publication Data
Warner, Jim, 1950-
    Facing pain—embracing love : the map to authentic living / Jim Warner. — 1st ed. — Boulder, CO : OnCourse International, c2009.
    p. (ill.) ; cm.
    ISBN: 9780615268576
    Includes bibliographical references.
    1. Self-actualization (Psychology)

BF637.S4 .W37 2009   158.1—dc22

2008911842

For Judy

I love you

Contents

Preface

As this first edition of *Facing Pain—Embracing Love* goes to press, our world is in crisis. We are confronting economic, environmental, and ideological challenges of unprecedented scale and gravity. Sadly, the noble focus of recent generations on progress, comfort, and our right to happiness has bred entitlement, greed, and isolationism. Consequently, we are now reeling from the worst worldwide recession in eighty years. We're finally acknowledging an ecological fragility that threatens the existence of life on our planet. Deepening ethnic conflicts and unconscionable terrorism sabotage the tenuous stability of major geopolitical regions and foment an ongoing and crippling global anxiety.

Safe havens no longer exist. Every human being on earth is affected. Most of us are scared. I know I am.

We can choose to view this fear as a catalyst for self-discovery and transformation. We can wake up from our stupor of indulgence and privilege, self-pity and blaming, and cynicism and judgment, and take full responsibility for our own actions and state of being. This angst urges us to probe the realities we usually resist—the difficult truths related to our identity, relationships, beliefs, and life purpose that fuel our confusion and depression.

It's time to face our pain.

For both nations and individuals, the era of "I can go it alone" has ended. It's time to accept that we need help and we need love—and we need one another. It's time to drop our façades of control and self-sufficiency, and give voice to our fears and vulnerabilities. It's time to fulfill our innermost longing to commune with others on an intimate, transparent level. It's time to give and receive compassion, kindness, forgiveness, appreciation, and support, without restrictions or agendas.

It's time to embrace love.

Our world is urgently calling upon us to grow. We need to move through our pain to a place of clarity and authenticity. We need to explore the frightening unknown of genuine fellowship. This book provides a map to guide us. There are no shortcuts, and shedding ingrained habits can be arduous. But, continuing to deny both our painful truths and our yearning to be loved will sentence us to a joyless, lonely existence.

Preface

We cannot change the world until we commit to changing ourselves. Let's decide to seize this pivotal moment in history to chart our own personal journey to truth and compassion. Then, as we reclaim our awareness and aliveness as individuals, we can work together to create a vibrant, loving world.

Acknowledgments

Many authenticity seekers assisted me in preparing *Facing Pain—Embracing Love*. I am grateful to:

My "Inspiration Team," who encouraged me during the conception and birthing of this book: Judy Wells Warner, Dave Bloom, and Kaley Klemp.

The illustration and editing team, who transformed a raw manuscript into flowing prose and pictures: Gillian Goodman, Kayla Morelli, Marco Morelli, Loma Huh, Sandra Jonas, Greg Summers, and John Drury.

The reviewers, all authenticity pilgrims, who challenged me and encouraged me to challenge and encourage others:

Catherine Bell	Michael Brown
Frank Buonanotte	Delynn Copley
Vince Corsaro	Jim Dethmer
Peter Evans	Rob Follows
Jim Glazer	Stephen Green
Ray Jefferson	Richie Kahn
Kelly Kelly	Jim Kochalka
Frieder Krups	James Sabry
Jeff Salzman	Margaret Smith
Jeff Snipes	Beat Steiner
Dave Trexler	Larry Trexler
Mark Tribus	Gunther Weil
Don Wrege	

Introduction

When Walt Disney animated Carlo Collodi's classic fable of transformation, *Pinocchio*, he magically brought to life the deepest longings of every human being: to be real and to experience love.

Over the past decade I've led hundreds of life-exploration retreats with executives and entrepreneurs (and their spouses) who came into the experience just as "wooden" as Collodi's puppet. These retreat participants came together to navigate difficult personal, vocational, and spiritual transitions. They shared several common laments: success without a sense of significance, listless relationships, gross time imbalances, and a general lack of grounding in their lives. Like Pinocchio, many had become virtual marionettes, twisting under the strings of a family history, corporate imperatives, or cultural mandates that demanded performance, wealth accrual, and recognition. They had hidden behind facades, duplicity, and pride. According to many retreat participants, their lives had been reduced to dancing on the stage of achievement (with occasional trips to their own version of Pinocchio's Pleasure Island). What was real? What was illusory? Many no longer knew. Their unconscious mantra had become "An actor's life for me."

Saddened to witness their struggles, I sought to develop a model for understanding the tensions, issues, and dreams of these supposedly successful people. I pondered, "What is the linkage between their yearning for comfort, their need to escape, and their core desire (at least in my judgment) to be present, aware, loving, supported, and real? How do these seemingly disparate longings and behaviors somehow fit together?"

Over time, after walking the introspective terrain with them for several years, I noticed a map of illusion and reality emerging. I began to see their journeys as a struggle to integrate two powerful and omnipresent life energies: Love and Pain. I believe authentic living requires us to reconcile these two energies, defining a framework for exploring and transforming complex, frustrating, and energy-draining life challenges. I offer you the Love↔Pain map as that framework.

This framework isn't just for high achievers, nor is it only for people under duress. For example, you may not be wealthy or move in elite circles, but in general, you are comfortable, blessed with loving relationships, grounded in your personal disciplines, and pretty much have your life together.

My reaction: Wonderful! Have gratitude! If this is true for you, view this book as *well care* for your whole being. Examine the impact of these two powerful energies on your life, and consider ways to achieve even greater personal awareness and deeper authenticity in your relationships. And if you're one of those high achievers wondering how to untangle the puppet strings of your life, you'll learn how to put the reins back in your own hands, so you, too, can deepen and expand your relationships and awareness.

Let's get started.

Facing Pain — Embracing Love

Mapping Love and Pain

The Love↔Pain model is presented here as a geographic metaphor, where the latitude represents a person's approach to Love, and the longitude represents his or her approach to Pain. An intersection point on the map represents a State of Being—for example, Playing Safe, Escape, Confusion, and Authentic Living. In the following pages, I describe how we move from state to state, and how we tend to get stuck in certain regions. You'll see that in the course of life, while we may wander all over the map, we tend to gravitate back to a particular state or region—over and over again.

My objective is to help you identify the general region on the map where you tend to reside (e.g., Numbness, Comfort, Isolation, or Authentic Living), understand the landscape of the different states, and assess the costs and consequences of the journey from where you are to the state of Authentic Living. The map is meant to clarify your general vicinity (let's say Kansas) more than to pinpoint your exact location (Main Street in Wichita). While I can give you the general directions toward Authentic Living, the turns and twists of your journey, including uncharted streams to ford and mountains to cross, will emerge as you travel. I offer no universal GPS that leads you directly to Authentic Living. Everyone's journey is unique. And you'll see the importance of having seasoned guides when you get lost in the

The States of Being Map

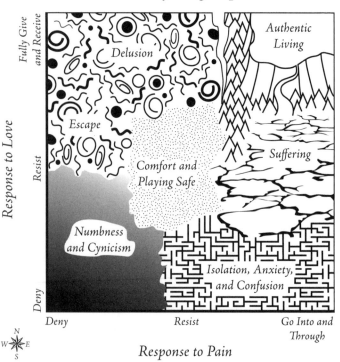

woods, lose your compass, or, like Pinocchio, find yourself in the belly of a whale.

One caveat: Even this geographic metaphor is imperfect, and I acknowledge that up front. As you'll discover, Authentic Living is not static. While I urge you to think of it as a desirable destination, I readily admit it is not a permanent location fixed on an immutable, perfectly drawn map. Nonetheless, imagined navigation through the Love↔Pain terrain is a useful—and potent—framework for your awareness journey.

You might ask, "Why Love and Pain?" My retreat experiences have repeatedly shown that we are always reacting to, or interacting with, these two potent forces. The intersection of these energies gives us a new reference point on our state of being—why we are *where* we are, and why we do *what* we do. You might find yourself in a particular state (perhaps Confusion) and wonder, "How did I get here?" By examining the map, you'll see how your approach to Love and your approach to Pain have led you to that state. Then you can assess the cost of shifting to a different approach that would lead you to a more fulfilling place.

The Love↔Pain Map also opens the lens on our spiritual life. This work has unapologetically spiritual underpinnings, where *spiritual* is defined as openness to, connection with, or communion with something larger than the self. Naming that "something" (God, Allah, Nature, Goodness, Universe, Holy Other, Awareness, Consciousness, or any other label you choose) is less important than your *openness* to it. My basic assumption is that this *desire* to connect or commune is intrinsic to every human being. It is the soul's deepest longing, the undercurrent of all life. Beliefs, traditions, cultures, values, and practices may vary, but this longing is common to all humanity.

The words *spiritual* or *religion* might be hot buttons for you. They may evoke memories, stories, judgments, projections, beliefs, or wounds that can narrow your openness and put you on the defensive. If this is true for you, I invite you to allow your *desire to connect* to outweigh any skepticism or reticence. Read on with curiosity, perhaps even a sense of wonder. Ultimately, Authentic Living requires both.

Definitions

A few other definitions provide bearings as you prepare to explore the map. Historically, many great teachers have offered varied and more expansive views on these concepts, so consider the following as alternatives rather than absolute definitions.

Ego is our need for recognition and validation separate from, independent from, or relative to others. It's the part of our identity that compares, measures, and judges. The Ego's mantras are "Life is about me," "Life happens to me," and "Life happens by me."

True Self is our identity as part of, in connection with, or in communion with all that is. It's the part of us that observes and appreciates, and is unattached to outcomes. The mantras of the True Self are "I am about life," and "Life flows through me."

Reality is whatever is happening right here, right now. This includes external events ("My niece has been injured in a car accident"), as well as any related thoughts ("How long will she be in the hospital? I wonder if she'll recover in time to return to school?"); emotions ("I'm angry at the driver . . . I'm afraid my niece won't recover fully"); bodily sensations (tears, muscle aches, or breaking out in hives); or behaviors (insomnia, irritability) we experience in reaction to these events. In other words, Reality is both the "outer truth" (the facts) about whatever is happening out there and our "inner truth" about whatever is happening inside ourselves as we observe or participate in life. Facts (the car was demolished and my niece is in the hospital) are part of Reality. Judgments (the driver is incompetent and they took my niece to the wrong hospital) are also part of Reality (our own private logic—whatever is "real" for us) and may or may not be true. The journey to Authentic Living requires us to separate facts from judgments. Reality invites us to acknowledge and accept the facts, while recognizing that our judgments are subjective.

Awareness is the act of observing, accepting, participating in, and experiencing whatever is happening in the moment, while not identifying with it. Awareness is being fully present to Reality.

Betrayal is the sense of abuse or desertion we experience when our vulnerability, openness, or trust has been violated by others.

Transactional Interaction refers to a *quid pro quo* relationship style, where our main concern is having our desires fulfilled, without making ourselves vulnerable to others. We may be friendly toward others, but our priority is getting what we want, physically, emotionally, or materially, in a calculated fashion, protecting against any downside. "I perform a service; you pay me. You perform a service; I compensate you." Transactional interactions put a governor on how much we will reveal to others or receive from others.

Authentic Interaction refers to an open, candid, and caring relationship with others, grounded in a genuine desire to connect transparently, free from pretense or deceit, understanding and embracing the fact that, in the purest sense, there is no separation between us.

With these definitions in mind, this book offers you a map of what you experience (your State of Being) based on how you choose to interact with the ever-present life dynamics of Love and Pain. The map helps you identify where you are at any moment (your current state). Residing in a particular State of Being *is your choice*—no one forced you there. It's up to you to make the conscious choice to move to a different location. My intent is to encourage you, perhaps inspire you, to seek the state of Authentic Living, achieved by your willingness, intention, and commitment to cross into—and all the way through—Pain, while fully giving and receiving Love.

The Love↔Pain Dimensions

The Pain Dimension

Pain is often defined as suffering or discomfort. Western culture teaches us to avoid pain, or alleviate it, if at all possible. Here, **Pain** is defined as any part of Reality we would prefer not to face: hard facts, mental or physical discomfort, fear, loss, death, "negative" feelings, and unrealized dreams. In essence it represents the uncomfortable truth about Reality.

Frankly, I've chosen the word *Pain* for the longitudinal axis of the map because it has more potency and wake-up power than other labels I considered. *Pain* grabs your attention. That said, if you have an aversion to using the word *Pain* on your own map, you may choose to substitute *Truth, Fear, Loss,* or *Reality*.

As you review the following definitions of the Pain dimension, consider as an example the "fact" that your mother has grown increasingly forgetful over the last two years.

> **Denying Pain** refers either to outright denial ("Mom's not forgetful" or "There's no problem here; Mom's fine") or to

total abdication ("I can't do anything about it, so I'm not even going to think about it").

Resisting Pain means acknowledging its existence while choosing not to address it: observing and avoiding the pain. When you resist pain, you might say things like, "My sister lives nearby; I'm sure she's on top of it," or, "I'll keep the conversations at a superficial level. There's no reason to test Mom's memory." In his landmark book, *The Road Less Traveled*, M. Scott Peck suggested that the greatest mental health issue our society faces is the drain from the energy we expend to *avoid* pain.[1]

Going Into and Through Pain means you are open to *all* of reality, without façades, excuses, or complaints. You face reality with an acceptance and awareness of all that *is*. Facing pain also implies taking responsibility for whatever is happening in your life. For example, your inner monologue might go something like this: "The doctor suspects that Mom has Alzheimer's. Why my mother?! I just got through teenage hell with my kids, and now I'm losing Mom. This stinks. *(Deep sigh.)* I already miss her. Okay, I've got to explore options for Mom, both medical care and her living situation. And I've got to face my own issues, too."

Facing pain is very different from *seeking* pain. Moving to the right (east) along the Pain dimension means both accepting and taking increased responsibility for whatever is happening in your life. Conversely, moving to the left (west) means greater detachment from, or denial of, whatever is happening in your life.

The Love Dimension

Love is defined here as communion with yourself, with others, and with a spiritual dimension, however you choose to define it. In different cultures and traditions, Love might mean grace, compassion, loving kindness, or connection with anyone or *anything*, including the natural world, and the supernatural or transpersonal world. Beyond the "enchantment love" romanticized in the media, this Love is a vulnerable, transparent communion.

> **Denying Love** is the refusal to connect in any vulnerable way. The basic, yet usually unspoken, philosophy of denying love is "I really don't need anyone. I choose to be on my own." All interactions are merely transactional.

> **Resisting Love** implies wanting the feel-good benefits of intimacy (pleasure, belonging), without the risk of betrayal ("I'm out to have a good time—no strings attached"). It means engaging in love only on your terms and conditions ("I don't let anyone get too close").

Fully Giving Love requires the transparent, vulnerable expression of all of yourself ("I offer all of myself to you").

Fully Receiving Love means having the openness and worthiness to welcome love and appreciation from others, however it is offered, and from the spiritual dimension, however you define this. It also means enjoying and

The Love↔Pain Axes

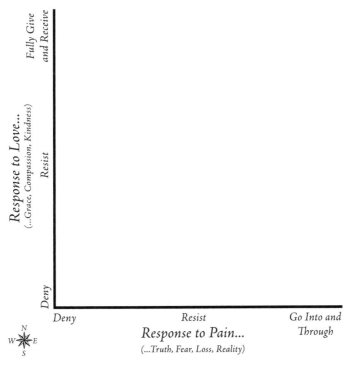

appreciating our possessions and the wonders of the natural world without attachment. "I open all of myself to receive all of you."

Giving and Receiving Love means the two-way experience of sharing grace, compassion, and kindness without measurement or comparison. It's as if our life is a *conduit* for love, where love flows into us from a source outside of us. As it flows through us, the love infuses us, permeates us, and replenishes us. And as it flows out of us, it carries the imprint of our True Selves, fully available to appreciate, honor, and nourish others.

Moving up (north) along the Love axis requires increasing openness, transparency, and vulnerability. Moving down (south) along the Love axis implies increased guardedness and stoicism, and an indifference or aversion to authentic interactions.

The State of Authentic Living— Begin with the End in Mind

Before exploring the other states, I want to give you a taste of **Authentic Living**. It's a state worthy of our striving. Later, we'll explore how to navigate here from the other states, and how to reside more fully in Authentic Living when the rest of your world conspires to pull you elsewhere.

Authentic Living is the paradoxical coexistence (not equality) of Love and Pain. Recall our definition of Reality as "what is," or the "truth." In Authentic Living, we experience Reality, celebrate it or weep with it, while not allowing it to overwhelm us. The mantra of Authentic Living might be "I accept things as they are, and I choose to love." Or, more simply, Authentic Living allows us to "Love what is."[2] We allow our Ego, with its need to compare and be seen, to recede so our True Self may emerge.

Authentic Living

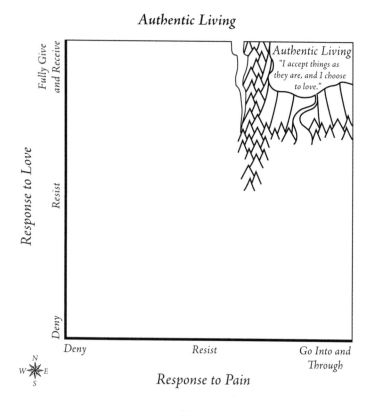

In Authentic Living, *joy* is experienced as the timeless, unmeasured "ahh-ness" of life, like receiving others' gratitude, appreciating a sunrise, or treasuring a newborn's smile. In contrast, *happiness,* or feeling good, is typically comparative ("This is the happiest day of my life") and time-bound ("I was happy yesterday, but not today"). Happiness is sought after, achieved, guarded, and lost. Joy just *is*.

Authentic Living demands an integrity and transparency that mirrors the acceptance and balance of both Pain and Love. The **Contrasting Behaviors** table on page 17 compares the common characteristics and behaviors of Authentic Living with those of other states. As you review the table, consider which behaviors of the other states reflect how you live your life *today*. Begin to ponder how these behaviors serve you, or even how you might enjoy them. Then reflect on how they breed anxiety, stunt your relationships, or otherwise constrain you. And finally, consider how your behaviors must change in order to experience Authentic Living.

We'll revisit this state of Authentic Living on page 70. This quick introduction should serve as a tempting glimpse into rich possibilities that can be yours. Hold this image of Authentic Living in mind as you assess your current state and contemplate your journey.

Contrasting Behaviors

Other States	The Authentic Living State
Blaming and complaining	Taking healthy responsibility for my life
Concealing	Candor and revealing
Maintaining a façade around feelings	Experiencing all feelings
Measurement and entitlement	Appreciation and gratitude
Defensiveness and control	Curiosity and collaboration
Withdrawal and indifference	Participation and courage
Comparing and seeking power	Equanimity and empowerment
Rescuing and caretaking	Caring and compassion
Being right	Learning, being present, and paying attention
Being smart or clever	Seeking knowledge and wisdom
Seeking achievement and accumulation	Joyful service and stewardship
Seeking notoriety	Presence
Finding the easy way	Discipline to do the hard thing
Resentment and vengeance	Forgiveness, compassion, and boundaries

The State of Comfort and Playing Safe

While many people *aspire* to the simplicity and peace of Authentic Living, most, especially in our affluent Western world, *settle* for the middle ground of **Comfort and Playing Safe**, resisting both Pain and Love. We acknowledge Pain, but avoid it if at all possible. We desire connection with others, but with clear limits. The bywords of Comfort are *control* and *comparison*. The Comfort mantra might be "Get security, be comfortable, stay in control."

In our twenties and thirties, during the make-my-mark stage of life (at least in Western culture), many of us are driven by a quest for happiness, material security, career advancement, and personal power. In this stage, we "play offense" in the competitive pursuit of financial security and recognition for our accomplishments. In so doing, we fall prey to the twin fallacies that "There is never enough" and "More is best." Later in life, in our forties, fifties, or sixties, when we have achieved some level of notoriety and material security, we switch to the preserve-and-protect mode and "play defense." We have entered the state of Comfort.

In Comfort, we measure achievements and relationships relative to some external standard, as if life is one big scoreboard. We're "better than," or "not as good as," but rarely "good enough." Friendships and intimate

Comfort and Playing Safe

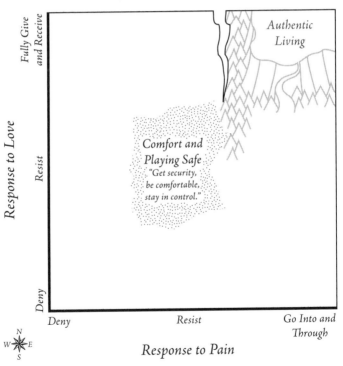

Authentic Living

Fully Give and Receive

Response to Love

Resist

Comfort and Playing Safe
"Get security, be comfortable, stay in control."

Deny

Deny   *Resist*   *Go Into and Through*

N
W   E
S

Response to Pain

relationships are fun, engaging, and pleasure filled, yet with some level of guardedness.

Furthermore, each of us has an inner **Risk Manager**.[3] It's the part of us that continually monitors situations and relationships, watching out for our physical and emotional safety. The Risk Manager maintains a data bank of the fear, shame, and betrayals accumulated over our lifetimes. Most of us developed our Risk Manager at an early age to play a key role in our lives: to help us avoid hurt. As a result, the Risk Manager closely monitors relationship intimacy, our exploration of the world, and how much we reveal of ourselves to others. Previous relationship betrayals make the Risk Manager ever more vigilant against future betrayals. The Risk Manager's credo is "We're not going to let *that* happen again!" We'll see later how honoring and "making a deal with" the Risk Manager is crucial if we aspire to Authentic Living.

In Comfort, our Risk Manager carefully monitors two things: which layers of ourselves we reveal to the world and our willingness to self-reflect and face difficult personal truths. As an example, consider your friendships. Perhaps you have fewer than you'd like.

Maybe you have none. Yet when asked in casual conversations about the breadth of your friendships, you may be prone to answer, "Oh, I'm lucky. I have lots of friends." The Risk Manager is simply doing his job: being polite and keeping you safe.

The **Layers of Truth** table shows how we behave (**Action**), depending on how deep into Truth we are willing to reside. In Comfort, we normally stay at the top two levels. The deeper we probe the reality of our situation (levels three and four), the closer we get to our genuine truth.

Layers of Truth

Level of Depth	Action	Related to Friendships	Related to Vocation
1	Deflect	"I have lots of friends."	"I have a great job."
2	Rationalize (no responsibility)	"I don't have time for friends."	"I perform a key role."
3	Explain (some responsibility)	"I don't reach out to make friends."	"It's important for me to stay busy."
4	Feel (the real truth)	"I feel abandoned, unworthy, and alone."	"I don't know what I really want to do."

When we reside in Comfort, few people (if any) are allowed access to our core truths. The more severe the betrayals experienced earlier in our lives, the more opaque our shrouding around the lower levels of our truth. Our Risk Manager's unspoken logic goes something like this: "If I open myself to speak my deeper truths, or fully experience love, I risk betrayal. Betrayal hurts. It's not worth the risk."

Even with this inner rationalization, most of us remain extremely high functioning in Comfort. We may hold a responsible job, be in a long-term relationship, and be pleasant to engage with. We probably appear confident, affable, successful, content, and happy. In the achievement-oriented parlance of the Western world, "We have made it."

Yet an inner voice tries to countermand our Risk Manager, reminding us, "This isn't *really* working . . . Surely there's more to life than *this*." A soft, yet continual, longing for a transcendent love keeps calling. Similarly, unspoken truths (feelings, secrets, resentments, and guilt over how we have hurt others) cloud our perception of Reality. Or we sense that something's not quite right: "I have so much to be thankful for—health, financial means, a fun family—what's wrong with me?" We don't want to appear ungrateful, so we resist the longings rather than face and explore them. As this inner voice grows louder and more persistent, we seek relief.

The State of Escape

This inner longing for more creates uneasiness in us, even though we are lodged in Comfort and Playing Safe. But, rather than face the truth of our longing, it's easier to retreat west along the Pain dimension into **Escape**. In this place of pain denial and lukewarm love, we salve our distress with diversions, pleasure, or addictive behaviors. Here, we fall prey to the implicitly sanctioned addictions of Western culture: power, money, luxury, recognition, and perpetual youthfulness. The media overtly endorses these as the accepted metrics for success or belonging. Alcohol, gambling and narcotics addictions, and the obsessive accumulation of possessions ("more stuff") are also prevalent among those seeking relief from a comfortable, yet disingenuous life.

As our love relationships languish, the yearning for intimacy, or at least sexual pleasure, can become desperate. Sexual escape manifests through pornography addiction, prostitution, or infidelity. Beyond the immediate pleasure, the secrecy of an extramarital affair can create a clandestine sanctuary in which we claim to connect and commune, while mocking Reality with our concealment and cover-ups.

Maintaining secrecy around our addictions takes guile and drains our energy. Nevertheless, the secrecy actually *serves* us by redirecting our attention from the loss of meaning or integrity in our lives. For example, covering up the cell phone charges and hotel receipts incurred when seeing a forbidden lover spares us from reflecting on how our career obsessions or raw selfishness have caused our marriage to go numb. Even maintaining the secrecy becomes a valued defense mechanism.

You may be thinking, "He must be referring to all the misfits of the world. I'm faithful to my spouse, I drink responsibly, I don't gamble, and I haven't smoked pot since my early twenties. I'm glad this doesn't apply to me." And while, in one sense, you may be right, consider that a fine line exists between personal relaxation or saw-sharpening habits and diversionary behaviors. Perpetually checking email, constantly monitoring your financial portfolio, immersing yourself in your kids' sports or studies, and obsessively fixating on physical

The States of Escape and Delusion

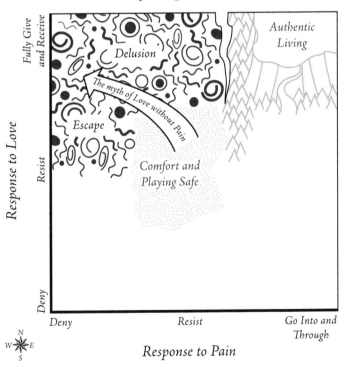

fitness or looking beautiful may be deflecting your attention from deeper, more meaningful, or more troubling life concerns.

The State of Delusion

The extreme form of escape is believing that Love can exist without Pain. This delusional image of a pain-free existence, bathing in pleasure, is a myth reinforced constantly in Western media—the illusion that we can "have it all" with minimal effort and no downside. When in **Delusion**, so-called loving relationships are supposedly "free," authentic, and mutual, while in reality they are totally transactional—solely for the purpose of satiating the egos involved. Love is no longer a gift, but an entitlement. Life becomes exclusively about me and my immediate gratification in the form of pleasure, power, or recognition.

Clichéd denizens of delusional hedonism or narcissism are aging athletes who stay in the game too long, and actors and rock stars who obsess over their looks into their eighties. Also common (and with more painful consequences for their constituencies) are the business, political, and religious leaders who become drunk with their own power, and live in the rarified air of position, absent any accountability. Inevitably, these people do something stupid (cheat on a spouse, make impossible promises, bundle and resell subprime loans, or alienate another head of state) and fall from power. Even after their folly or deceit is uncovered, many remain in denial. Certain past presidents and financial tycoons may come to mind. Their denial or defiance often leads to a media circus, confusion among their faithful, and a general fallout that can take years to abate.

People in this extreme state of escape enjoy *sensations* (substance-induced euphoria, the rush of the deal, or absolute control over others), but they don't actually *feel* their emotions (fear, sadness, or even joy). They mistake sensation for feeling, eroticism for intimacy, and power for presence, believing, "Whatever is good for me is good for all." Because they are delusional, these hedonistic, selfish, or narcissistic people eventually experience a shattering fall. Please take note: Caring for hedonists, narcissists, and others living in Delusion will simply enable and perpetuate their behavior. *If you know and care for such people, your first priority must be to take care of yourself.*

Insulating Yourself from Narcissistic or Delusional People

- Detach your own well-being from their well-being.

- If they recover—great; if they don't, it is by their choice.

- Once you are detached from the outcome, arrange an intervention (the narcissist or addict won't like it, but it may save his or her life).

- Set and enforce your personal boundaries, so that their behaviors don't diminish your well-being. In this way, when they do fall, you can be direct and compassionate in your support.

- Be prepared for the relationship to end. They may reject, ostracize, or even persecute you. But if you continue to ignore or enable their delusion, you only postpone their inevitable, and likely harsh, encounter with Reality, and compromise your own well-being.

The State of Isolation, Anxiety, and Confusion

After a while in Escape or Delusion, many people again experience the inner voice whispering, or sometimes bellowing, "Your life isn't working; you are a fraud; WAKE UP!" This wake-up call often triggers an abrupt descent into **Isolation, Anxiety, and Confusion**. It's the hangover after the high. In this state of high pain and little love, confronted with our own uncertainty or even helplessness, we may feel adrift, lost, guilty, ashamed, and alone. And the longer the time we spent locked in Escape or Delusion, the deeper and longer our fall into anxiety and perhaps depression. Unfortunately, we reap what we sow. Consider the following examples.

Sam has devoted the past twenty years to building his career, achieving position, power, and wealth. Most of the time, he thrived on the pressure. And when the pace became too intense, he'd buy another toy or have a weekend fling. But the constant travel and grueling pace have taken their toll. Now in his mid-forties, he and his wife endure a listless marriage, and his teenagers have become both belligerent and entitled. His latest physical revealed early-stage diabetes, the price of his life of excess. When he tried to open conversation with some associates about his sense of malaise, they laughed it off as Sam's "midlife crisis." On a recent plane ride, reflecting on the state of his life, his stomach became so knotted he couldn't eat. He feels lost.

Julia rose quickly in her career and loves the varied challenges and responsibilities of her job. She also relishes her roles as a mother of two young children and as chairwoman of a local nonprofit. Divorced for three years, she has enjoyed a romantic connection with Perry for the past eighteen months. However, Perry's career demands both extensive travel and regular social engagements, which he expects Julia to attend. Their intimate moments are rare, as most of their couple time is devoted to kids' events or calendar matching. Her life has become a constant juggling act, balancing her varied life demands with taking time for herself. Yet she's often wracked with guilt over shortchanging her kids, her romantic partner, her work, and her friends.

Outwardly, many of us have learned to mask our

feelings, keeping them secret from even those closest to us. In so doing, we find ourselves caught in a double bind: the pain of our internal angst ("The secrecy and duplicity around my affair is eating me up") and the need to maintain an outward façade ("My clients, friends, neighbors,

The State of Isolation, Anxiety, and Confusion

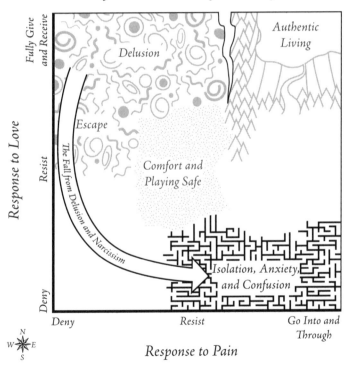

and church would disown me if they knew my secret").

As our anxiety and confusion escalate, we might turn to medications (e.g., anti-anxiety drugs) to move west on the Pain axis and a little north into the Comfort and Safety state. These medications can offer temporary relief, but not a cure. Sometimes this respite can be positive, allowing us to regroup, perhaps initiate some deeper life reflection, and assemble a support community in preparation for a more intentional Journey to Authentic Living. However, there's a risk they will become a way-of-life compromise, limiting the depth of our anxiety or depression, yet also placing a governor on our ability to feel and be truly alive.

At first the painful truth of Isolation, Anxiety, and Confusion reminds us of Escape's folly. We recall that denial always has a price. With this insight we return to Comfort, intent on being more prudent and discerning: "I've learned my lesson. I now know my boundaries."

Often, however, the lessons learned in Isolation, Anxiety, and Confusion are short lived. Comfort becomes boring. Escape activities beckon, and we again enter the orbit between Escape and Isolation. This orbit might look like the following: "Wow, I had no idea paying off the credit card debt would take so long. But, finally, that's over. Gee, did you see the deals they're offering on the new model cars? They've really improved the mileage, and resale values are high. We haven't

The Escape/Isolation Orbit

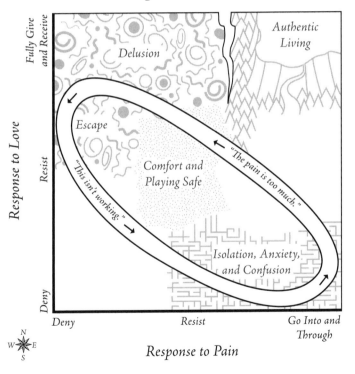

done anything nice for ourselves in a long time." The rationalization wins, and you buy the car, return to debt, and repeat the cycle.

Orbits Around the Comfort State

After a few laps on the Escape-Isolation circuit, the more mature yet guarded of us rein in our desires and retreat to the safety of Comfort. We then tend to cycle in a tighter orbit, held in the gravitational protection of Comfort and Security ("Okay, that's enough of the new cars. We'll live with the Toyota for a few years"), while occasionally testing the edges of Escape ("Hey, did you see the deals they're offering on excursions to Turkey?"). These dalliances into Escape inevitably spiral us back into Confusion and Anxiety ("What were we thinking when we bought those gemstones at the bazaar?"), just not as severely as they did before. We live again in the moderation of Comfort, but now from the stance of "playing defense"—protecting our possessions, our image, and our ego, rather than risking our safety or sanity through overindulgence and its resultant crash. The following internal monologue is typical:

"I make a decent living. But we need to put aside money for the kids' college. So we have to watch expenses. But we still need to finish the basement. On the other

The Comfort State Orbit

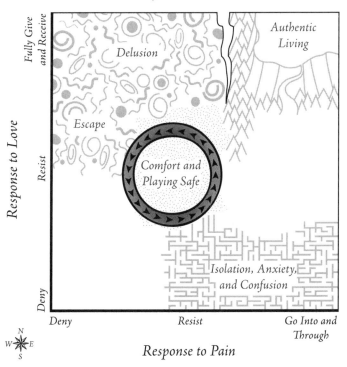

hand, what if the markets go down again? Maybe we need to redo our portfolio allocations. We're healthy now and could save some money with a higher deductible on our health care. But what if we have a major accident?"

This constricting Comfort orbit creates ongoing, low-grade, seesaw anxiety—the nagging sense that something's not quite right ("I'm doing all the right things. How come I still feel so lousy?"). Tension amplifies when we catch glimpses of others who live primarily in Authentic Living—reminding us of what we could have in our own lives if we weren't so selfish or defensive ("How can *he* be so upbeat? Nothing seems to faze him. I don't get it. I make more money. I live in a nicer home. My kids go to better schools. I should be happier!").

We long for the happiness and fulfillment beyond merely protective Comfort. But having tasted the pain of Anxiety, we fear the vulnerability that's required for Authentic Living. The Risk Manager's rationalization takes over. This time our inner monologue might be, "I like my stuff. It's not so bad here. If I have the difficult conversation with my boss (father, neighbor, or lover), I could get fired (disowned, shunned, or abandoned)." Or "I'd love to teach, but there's not enough money in it to support my lifestyle. We'd have to downsize. Besides, maybe I'm a better business person than teacher. I don't know how it will turn out. Better not risk it." Or "I think I'll just sit tight. I'll be okay. There are a lot of people worse off than I am."

So we spin in the cocoon of Comfort, battling the voices in our heads, resisting the pain of an authentic life shift, and imposing a governor (that trusty Risk Manager) on the depth and intimacy of our relationships. After a few spins, the comfort and material security become so powerful, we're no longer even resisting pain or love. We simply lose the capacity to tap into either, often in a quiet resignation: "I guess that's just the way it is." And this is when we start to go numb.

The State of Numbness and Cynicism

For many people, the unstable orbit around Comfort gradually devolves into the southwest quadrant of the Love↔Pain map, **Numbness and Cynicism**. This state represents a denial of both love and truth, a soul-level void of being. Our inner longings are still present, just entombed in denial, rationalization, bitterness, or victimhood. In Cynicism, we take little responsibility for our own lives, especially our own malaise. All fault for our discontent resides *out there*, as our interactions with others become a litany of blaming and complaining.

In this state, our relationships become perfunctory or transactional, and we avoid any contact in which we might become vulnerable. Life is staged, calculated, executed, and bemoaned, but not *lived*.

Here's an example of Numbness and Cynicism: Envision a couple in their midsixties meandering into the country club for Sunday brunch. As they sit down, he complains to his crony at the adjacent table about the messy locker room, poorly groomed golf course, and general incompetence of the city council. She complains that her coffee is too cold, the eggs are too runny, and the service is too slow. After they eat in silence, they return home. He reads the business section of the paper, while she watches TV or reads a magazine. Dialogue between them, if there is any, centers around the inconvenience of next week's doctor visits and complaints that their children never call. In the evening, they'll have several cocktails with friends, yet again reliving collegiate escapades or planning next year's trip abroad. Their solace comes from recalling past experiences or imagining future hopes. They either ignore or revile the realities of the present.

The universe constantly offers wake-up calls, even to those residing in Numbness and Cynicism. They typically come in the form of celebrations (birth of a grandchild) and crises ("major" birthday, death of a family member, shattered marriage, financial devastation, or debilitating injury or accident). Yet we can view even these with sarcasm, stoicism, or resignation: "Oh, isn't your new granddaughter cute! I'll bet college tuition will cost you a fortune when she grows up," or "Over fifty percent of marriages end in divorce anyway. It was wrong from the start. What can you do?"

As we spiral deeper into the hole of Numbness, we become increasingly rigid and judgmental toward others ("I know what I'm doing. Leave me alone. They're

Slipping into Numbness and Cynicism

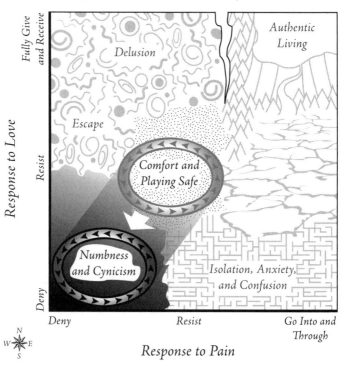

all idiots"). We're prone to defiance and anger toward supposed friends who get too close to our inner emptiness. ("You don't know what you're talking about!" or "Don't give me all this touchy-feely psychobabble.") Our relationships become mechanical and utilitarian, lacking variety and tenderness. We avoid all but perfunctory, transactional relationships. When thrust into potentially vulnerable or intimate environments, our first reaction is to close down completely.

Many of us in Numbness suffer from "chronic love deficiency," unable or unwilling to connect at the heart level with the world, with ourselves, or with the Divine. As an antidote, we adopt an aura of invincibility, deflecting or rejecting others who seek to connect, while demeaning those who seem weak and vulnerable. The desire to compare and control that characterized us in Comfort devolves into an obsession with sanctimony in Numbness. Perhaps the saddest aspect of Cynicism is a feeling of disdain or even hatred toward innocent, spontaneous people, who smile a lot and seemingly don't get hung up in either their own cares or the cares of the world. We might judge them as shallow, unrealistic, stupid, or childish. Their aliveness threatens the barricades around our own walled-off longings. In one sense, our disgust for present, aware people is a projection of our own confusion and self-loathing. Ironically, the people we most disdain could be our best guides out of Numbness and into a life of feeling.

The Journey to Awareness and Authentic Living

Even when caught in the throes of Cynicism and Numbness, embers of our True Self always exist and hunger for expression. We need a breakthrough: a jump start into the **Journey to Awareness**. The breakthrough may begin with the simple recognition "My life isn't working, and I'm committed to exploring why." Or "I sense I'm just skimming the surface of life. I'm committed to more depth and authenticity." More often, it's triggered by a jolting external crisis (e.g., sudden death of a loved one or financial devastation) or a spiritual epiphany. There's a sense of readiness: a head, body, and heart openness to an unvarnished view of our True Self and a more intentional and transparent life. It's not a commitment to do anything yet—just a willingness to explore and understand the vexing issues that keep us stuck. To paraphrase Step One of the Recovery Movement's Twelve-Step Program,[4] healing starts with this admission: "[Either by emotional inability or by catastrophic event], I'm powerless to resolve the issues on my own. My life has become unmanageable. I need help."

Most of us stuck in Comfort, Numbness, or Confusion want to make a beeline for the northeastern state of Authentic Living. But before going "upward and outward," we must go "downward and inward." We must face, embrace, and transform the parts of ourselves we have denied or resisted. Like Pinocchio, we must come to terms with the lies we keep telling ourselves in order to maintain the illusion of our okay-ness. In navigating the Love↔Pain terrain, this means we must willingly go east, and often southeast, into and through our pain, even when we feel hopeless doing so. The longer and more vehemently we've denied pain and love, the longer and deeper our descent. This is when the Outward Bound[5] motto most applies: "When you can't get out of it, get into it."

Whether coming from Comfort, Escape, or Numbness, we're now at a pivotal juncture represented by the starburst symbol in the figure **Examples of the Journey**. We may have been in Isolation, Anxiety, and Confusion

Examples of the Journey

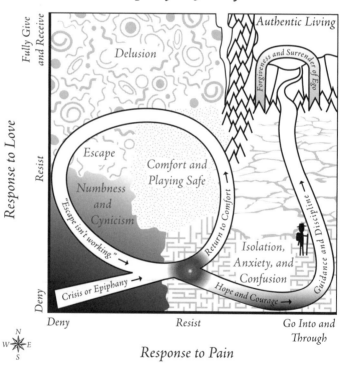

Response to Pain

for a while, with no end in sight. We want some relief, and it's oh so tempting to return to Comfort.

I've resisted this eastward part of the journey multiple times in my own life, looking for easy ways out (or up). And I've advised hundreds of successful, comfortable people looking for a quick journey—the helicopter ride over the crevasses to Authentic Living. From my own journey and my work with others, I've concluded the following: Quick fixes don't last. We may feel good for a time, but sustained authenticity, in all areas of life, means committing to self-exploration, going into and through the difficult truths and emotions we have denied or resisted. There are no shortcuts.

A Guide for the Journey

Wise mountain climbers or river rafters, exploring terrain for the first time, retain seasoned guides who have already scaled the peaks or navigated the rapids. These guides know the risks of the journey and the fulfillment and exhilaration at its end. They also know the exact places *en route*, where new adventurers may tend to be too bold when the risks are high, or falter when only a little more perseverance would allow them to surmount an obstacle. Guides know when to challenge and when to encourage; when to be flexible and when to draw boundaries; when to push on when the goal is near; and when to retreat, reflect, regroup, and rest when adventurers are exhausted.

Likewise, your eastward journey into resisted truths calls for a guide: a professional coach, counselor, mentor, therapist, advisor, sponsor, spiritual director, or friend. These guides will listen and care, offering neither judgments nor quick solutions. Choose experienced guides who have navigated, and continue to navigate, their own awareness journeys. Their role is to provide the encouragement, compassion, discipline, and accountability needed to help you navigate your own denied realities.

Seasoned guides shine the light of truth and affirmation on your personal pain. Having made the journey for themselves, they can forewarn you of drifts back into your old behaviors and can encourage you to keep going, to face, explore, and transform all you have avoided or denied. Without these human guides, you may be overcome by hopelessness, wander in the maze of Isolation and Anxiety, or revert back to Comfort and Playing Safe or Numbness and Cynicism.

Once you truly commit to your journey, candidate guides will begin to appear in your life. As they appear (a speaker you hear at a conference, a professional coach referred by a friend, an author whose work you admire, or a co-worker who exudes calmness and compassion during times of crisis), *you*, the protégé, are responsible for approaching them, the mentors, inviting their support and guidance. It's a courageous and vulnerable move, and you may experience some rejection. This is where you must also begin to demonstrate hope—the vital belief in unrealized goodness that undergirds all change.

Getting Started on the Journey

Take comfort. The first step out of Numbness or Comfort into the pain of our denied realities doesn't have to be an all-or-nothing leap. It may be a simple desire to understand, "How and why did I get here?" Movement into and through denied emotions like anger, fear, and grief may evolve more slowly, depending on the depth

What to Look For in Authentic Living Guides

- They have a way of being you admire. They walk their talk.

- Their lives are grounded in grace, truth, compassion, patience, and discipline.

- They are neither intimidated nor intimidating. They are unflappable under duress.

- They have the presence and wisdom to know when to stay in the background and let things unfold, and when to be decisive in the moment.

- They can quickly get to the heart of problems and speak the hard truths.

- They can "hold the space" for you to express your truth and emotions safely.

- They treat confidentiality as a sacred trust.

- They are committed to their own ongoing personal growth and holistic health.

- They have their own "personal advisory board" for guidance and accountability.

- They are spiritually grounded and committed to ongoing spiritual practices or disciplines.

- Their work is about you, not them. As such, they "lead from a step behind."

of our denial, our general emotional awareness, and the experience and presence of our guides. Fellow seekers committed to self-discovery and self-transformation provide mutual encouragement on the journey eastward.

Many people ask, "So, how long will this take?" while inwardly concluding, "Okay, I guess I can do this once and be done with it." Not so. Sustained awareness is a lifelong commitment. Consider the following analogy from Western medicine:

Every twelve to eighteen months, I visit a preventive health-care specialist for a full-body CT scan and a full blood workup. He then pokes and explores every orifice on my body, and carefully examines every square inch of my skin. After that, we sit at a computer where he patiently walks me through every part of my body, celebrating what's working well and identifying every anomaly. He then offers his recommendations and we collaborate on what to do about the areas of concern.

In the same way, the journey to Authentic Living begins with a "full-life CT scan" (see Appendix A for an abbreviated example of this scan), followed by explicit prescriptions and disciplines to acknowledge, accept, and transform those areas of our lives that drain our energy and compromise our aliveness.

In my case, I have heart disease. It is not what I wanted to hear from my doctor. But I'd prefer to know now and take immediate and bold steps to alter my lifestyle (reduce fat intake, add daily nutritional supplements, take statins to manage cholesterol, and undergo regular stress tests), rather than drop dead out of ignorance or denial. I have committed to doing whatever it takes to have the healthiest heart (as well as lungs, organs, bones, and brain) possible.

Most people resonate with this "I want to know" mind-set about their bodies. Imagine having the same approach to your psycho-spiritual well-being and your relationship authenticity. Wouldn't you want to know where you are unhealthy (out of balance, out of integrity) in these areas, and then commit to doing whatever it takes to regain full emotional, interpersonal, and psycho-spiritual health?

And, like my regular visits to the health-care specialist and my ongoing heart-care disciplines, sustained Authentic Living requires both constant vigilance (scanning my life for energy drains and inauthentic behaviors) and daily well-care practices (solitude time, small group accountability, and service to others). I want to reinforce: This is a lifelong commitment.

Action Steps on the Journey

We've seen that the journey to Authentic Living starts with an admission of your powerlessness, your commitment to change, and your willingness to enlist support.

Additional Tips for Getting Started

- Make an inventory of the difficult conversations you have been avoiding.
- Make an inventory of what you like about yourself.
- Make an inventory of your gratitudes.
- Make an inventory of what's missing in your life, what you are tolerating, with whom you are out of integrity, your longings, and how you sabotage yourself.
- Read contemporary "Awareness" authors (see Appendix F).

Then it demands that you take complete and full responsibility for whatever is happening in your life. "I have heart disease." (Or "My relationship with my spouse / child / parent / friend is unhealthy.") "It's a reality. No one 'did this to me.' Yes, I'm upset, sad, and scared, and I don't know how this will end up. But I take full responsibility both for my situation and for my recovery."

Stop the excuses, blaming, and complaining. You are committed to and responsible for whatever is happening in your life. Only when you take full responsibility for your life do you have the opportunity for sustained transformation.

Responsibility also requires identifying the withheld truths and covert actions that have hurt either you or others. In a sense, this is an examination of conscience and can include a confession to another human being about all your actions or relationships that cause you to be out of integrity with yourself or others.[6] In this step, you reveal past actions and relationships that have derailed your integrity. This difficult assignment is likely to make you feel vulnerable. You may be tempted to look for an easy way out, perhaps a quick return to Comfort, which beckons and is always available. Instead, choose to get it all out on the table. Look your truth in the face. In addition to this confession, you might invite a friend or relative who knows you well to share his or her concerns about your life.

Remember that the longer you've denied or resisted your truth, the more raw and painful its revelation. It will likely be unpleasant to experience your shame over belittling your spouse's idiosyncrasies; your feelings of abandonment when recalling how your parents weren't there for you in childhood; your potential rejection by others when you choose to have the difficult conversations instead of "playing nice."

One follow-up to this moral inventory is to make amends with those you have hurt or betrayed by your actions. Reparation is at the heart of Step Nine of the Twelve-Step Program,[7] and invites you to approach those you have hurt, asking them what must to be done to clear the slate. It can be as simple as asking for forgiveness, or—more courageously—asking, "What can I do to get back into integrity with you?" Sometimes the other person will also want to clear the slate, and you'll collaborate on either reconciliation or clean closure. Other times, they'll ignore or vilify you, essentially closing off the relationship. Either way, you have at least made the overture with the sincere desire to repair or close the relationship cleanly.

No doubt, this is hard work. Fortunately, just as joining a health club and retaining a personal trainer can accelerate your return to physical health, you can stay on course toward Authentic Living by bonding with a small group of fellow pilgrims, attending personal growth workshops and seminars, and enlisting experienced guides. These approaches provide hope and encouragement that the journey is worth its price. Your community may be a spiritual fellowship, a recovery-movement meeting group, or any gathering of honest, loving friends who will tell you the truth, illuminate your blind spots, and help you stay tethered to your values. Appendix C offers an example vision statement and guidelines for this type of small group.

Relationship Clarity

The Journey to Authentic Living also requires knowing what to leave behind. We must acknowledge the relationships that may at one time have been intimate or important, but have since become either transactional or hurtful. These relationships might include a controlling business partner, a bitter ex-spouse, an interfering in-law, a smothering friend, a fawning subordinate, or a cynical employee. Get clear with yourself about what you want out of these relationships, and about the investment you are willing to make to get it.

You might accept that certain relationships are transactional, and then, by expressing your own truths and vulnerabilities, seek to move those relationships to a more authentic, intimate level. It's a risky move that may lead to degradation or even dissolution of the relationship. On the other hand, you may achieve a satisfying breakthrough that would never have happened without your making the first move. For example, you might approach a business partner with whom you feel duress, asking her, "I notice I'm feeling some tension in our relationship.

I feel sad that we've lost the sense of collaboration that once made us a great team. I regret I haven't approached you on this before. And now, I'd welcome the opportunity for us just to sit and talk. I'm very open to hearing what's coming up for you, about me and about our relationship." There's a risk she may discount or belittle you. Or, this could be the opening she needed to heal a multi-year rift and start a fresh relationship.

Occasionally, you may choose to stay in a transactional or even draining relationship—for example, an ex-spouse with whom you share child custody or a relative you see only at family reunions. You've determined that the potential fallout from a confrontation (whipsawed kids or family drama) isn't worth the cost. Staying authentic in these difficult relationships often means adopting an attitude of compassion for others, while protecting the boundaries of your sanity. As you consider the other person(s), your self-talk might go something like, "I'm sad this relationship didn't work out the way I wanted. I own my part in the tension in the relationship. I choose to be pleasant and cordial with you in the effort to achieve our common goal (raise healthy kids or retain some semblance of family harmony). And if I feel my own sanity and presence are being compromised, I will politely set boundaries and take care of myself."

Sometimes, after repeated attempts at collaboration or reconciliation, you may determine that a more transparent relationship is not possible. You may then consciously choose to end the relationship or simply let it die. Often, these relationships will expire on their own when you cease making any proactive contact. However, be prepared for the person to approach you and ask, "Hey, what's up? I'm trying to contact you and you are either always busy or don't return my calls. Are you avoiding me?" The authentic response at this point is to speak your truth, compassionately, yet firmly, and no matter how painful, to the person. Your don't-rock-the-boat Risk Manager often intervenes at this point, urging you to "play nice" and withdraw to Comfort, Numbness, or Escape, rather than have the difficult encounter. If you've made your decision to end the relationship, go east into your truth, and end it. If this is a new experience for you, Appendix D offers guidance on how to end a relationship.

Getting clear on the state of your relationships is a key part of your authenticity audit and the journey northward to Authentic Living. The Whole-Life Relationship Audit in Appendix B offers a quick litmus test on the health of your most important life relationships.

The State of Suffering

Once you allow your facades to begin falling away, and you experience the painful reality of all you have denied, you may feel an emotional torrent as fear, anger, and sadness escalate. As you come clean with others, apologizing and making amends, they may reject or abandon you. Often, reflection on your past transgressions can trigger waves of guilt and shame. These might lead to a sense of heroic suffering or martyrdom as you endure your well-deserved punishment. Conversely, resentment, vengeance, or even rage may emerge, directed either at yourself—for your past actions—or at others who have hurt you. At some point you may actually begin to identify with the pain ("I *am* guilty. I *am* shameful. I *am* an angry person"). This shame-martyrdom-rage combination can be a potent and debilitating emotional cocktail.

You may be tempted to wallow in this state of **Suffering**, blaming others (unforgiveness) or shaming yourself (unworthiness and self-flagellation). It's like having cancer and believing you *are* the cancer. The combination of unforgiveness and unworthiness can create devolving orbits of hopelessness and resignation ("It's too hard. What's the use?") that can spiral you back into variations of the Escape-Isolation-Numbness orbit.

Internal anguish will occasionally manifest outwardly in what appear to be positive actions, like battling social injustice. While participation in a group service mission may be a facet of your healing journey, it can sometimes become twisted, leading you right back into the old patterns you were trying to shed. Here's how: You channel your repressed resentment toward perpetrators, or your shame over past transgressions, into "making a difference in the world." You rationalize, "If I can't get even with the people who hurt me or make amends to the people I hurt, I'll devote myself to an altruistic cause (addressing world hunger, building third-world schools)." Even this motive can be sabotaging. We risk using seemingly noble actions as a way of assuaging guilt, or throw ourselves into causes almost militantly as an indirect way of "getting even" with our perpetrators. The danger here is that we subsume our identity either in the success of the cause

The Suffering Orbit

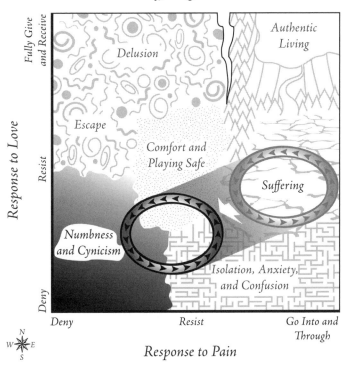

or in how much we can endure for the cause as penance for past sins, either ours or the perpetrator's.

Ironically, holding on to resentment or guilt is yet another insidious form of control. Clinging to them, even in the guise of the do-gooder, creates barriers that block our ability to (1) receive love from others ("Remember what happened last time? Don't get hurt again"); (2) love ourselves ("You need to suffer for what you did; you can't let it go"); and (3) forgive others ("Make them pay for what they did"). Hanging on to unforgiveness, resentment, or vengeance toward others is like drinking poison and waiting for the other person to die.[8]

In these cases, your Journey to Authentic Living has stalled. After bravely venturing into the internal torrent of your pain, you are in danger of becoming caught in the vortices of resentment, martyrdom, and unworthiness.

Forgiveness and Letting Go

Caught in the whirlpool of resentment, martyrdom, and unworthiness, you are nevertheless poised at the gateway to Authentic Living. But how to proceed? Where to go now? Recalling the "play offense" period of achievement in the Comfort state, and encouraged by your persistent and compassionate guides, you realize unforgiveness and unworthiness no longer serve you. A new realization emerges: "This isn't working. Maybe I don't need these anymore. What can I do to release them? How do I push my way into peace and joy?"

The answer is perhaps your most difficult realization, especially for competitive, just-figure-it-out, high achievers: *You must simply let go and receive.* To paraphrase the Tao of Leadership[9]:

> When you let go of what you are, you become what you might be.
>
> When you let go of what you have, you receive what you need.

Pinocchio modeled this when he willingly gave his own wooden, donkey-ears-and-tail life to save his father. By this ultimate surrender—metaphorically, the drowning of his ego—his authentic self was free to emerge in the form of a real, flesh-and-blood boy.

Similarly, you are invited to allow the final release of *your* controlling ego. And the stay-in-control ego typically doesn't surrender without a fight. Yet only from a place of surrender and trust in something larger than yourself are you ready to embrace love fully and accept reality graciously. For most of us, letting go will be counterintuitive. It's the opposite of what we have done our entire lives.

Because the concepts of surrender and reliance on others may be foreign to you, this is where experienced guides can help you most. They'll show you that, in

Authentic Living, no terms are placed on love, no *quid pro quos*. Authentic love is unconditional. All you need to do is release and receive.

This surrender of ego requires a *disconnection* from the strictures of Comfort and Playing Safe that may have served you for a lifetime. These include control,

The Final Gateway

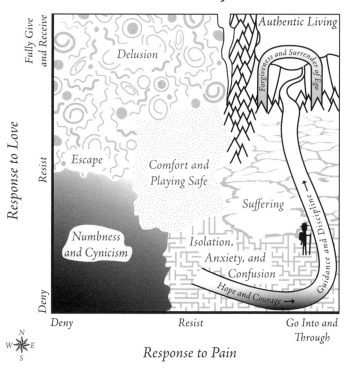

Response to Love

Fully Give and Receive · Resist · Deny

Authentic Living

Forgiveness and Surrender of Ego

Delusion

Escape

Comfort and Playing Safe

Suffering

Numbness and Cynicism

Isolation, Anxiety, and Confusion

Guidance and Discipline

Hope and Courage →

Response to Pain

Deny · Resist · Go Into and Through

N · W · E · S

comparison, measurement, independence, and material security. It's like you are swinging on a rickety trapeze bar that represents your ego. It's comfortable, familiar, and going nowhere. And you have to kick and push just to keep the bar moving. Ahead of you, foggy in the distance, is another trapeze bar representing your True Self and Authentic Living. You must release the comfort and familiarity of the current bar, float through the void between the bars, and grasp onto a new, transformed life adventure. Any major life transformation boils down to the same basic question: Are you willing to let go of one bar to reach the next?[10]

Forgiveness is a required part of letting go. Forgiveness means granting yourself an unconditional pardon, and also one to those who have betrayed you. It means refusing the poison of resentment and vengeance. Only through forgiveness do you open yourself to receive the unconditional pardon (and love), both from others and also from a transcendent, loving Spiritual force (energy, entity, being, space), whatever you perceive that to be. Granting forgiveness, loving ourselves, and receiving others' love dissolves the mind-set of separation, isolation, and independence that governs the dualistic "me versus them" universe. This is usually a scary process, though typically cathartic, emotional, and cleansing. Forgiveness, coupled with a belief in your own worthiness to receive love—without having to do anything in return—births (or rebirths) you into your True Self and an Authentic Life.

Rarely does this forgiveness happen all at once. Typically, there are moments of explicit forgiveness, periods of acceptance, and occasional drifts back into resentment. When this happens, go easy on yourself. These drifts are natural. For example, you may feel you've forgiven the teens who taunted you mercilessly in adolescence. But every now and then, you flash back to the humiliation or to the abuse. Your heart races as you re-experience the shame, and then you play out vengeance scenarios in your head.

As you acknowledge the desire for revenge—perhaps even enjoy it for a moment—and then gently release the flashback feelings, you'll find they become less frequent until you are no longer hooked by past incidents or individuals. Often a ritual (writing—and then burning—a letter, or performing a mock burial) can serve as a powerful release, as you process the layers of forgiveness. Ritualistic processes are typically emotional, cleansing, and transformative.

You might be thinking, "Okay, I get it. Makes sense. How does this actually happen?" Here again, seasoned guides will help you chart your initial path, based on your unique history and capacities. This is similar to river guides planning an assault on the final bank of Level Five rapids. The whitewater is frothy, you're already exhausted from the journey, you remember being caught in earlier eddies, and it's getting dark. Guides will encourage you to trust the innate navigation skills of your re-emerging True Self, and stay the course.

Working with your guides, you'll craft your own self-reflection habits and healing rituals. Whatever approaches you choose, the objective is to release yourself from the toxic resentments and shame that block your entry into Authentic Living. While the steps are necessary to *become* Authentic, we'll see in a moment that they are not sufficient to *sustain* Authentic Living.

Tools for Navigating
Unforgiveness and Unworthiness

- List the attributes you admire about yourself.

- List the attributes you admire about your betrayers (this definitely takes some courage!).

- Make an inventory of all the ways you express defensiveness in your life. For example:

  - Communicating with righteous indignation and spitefully demanding evidence

  - Feigning polite interest, while inwardly clinging to your point of view and/or rehearsing your rebuttal

- Consciously replace defensive behaviors with genuine curiosity. For example:

  - View every interaction as a learning experience

  - Express sincere wonder and interest in others' viewpoints

  - Feel and show genuine enthusiasm about the possibilities of others' ideas

- Invite friends and loved ones to verbalize their appreciation and love for you, and limit your response to simply, "Thank you."

Authentic Living—
A View from the Inside

Consider that Authentic Living is more a vista than a destination, more an unfolding mystery than a permanent solution. With that understood, two important approaches to Authentic Living stand out: **Unattachment**, holding but not clinging, enjoying but not possessing; and **Equanimity**, the acceptance of Reality without comparison or measurement. The Sufi mystic Rumi beautifully characterizes these two concepts as a means for reunion with our True Self:

> *The day will come when, with elation,*
> *you will greet yourself arriving at your own door*
> *in your own mirror*
> *and each will smile at the other's welcome,*
> *saying: "Sit here, eat."*
> *You will love again the stranger who was yourself.*
> *Give wine, give bread,*
> *give back your heart to itself,*
> *to the stranger who has loved you all your life,*
> *whom you ignored for another,*
> *who knows you by heart.*[11]

Authentic Living embodies the lifelong paradox of simultaneously giving and receiving love, while facing and accepting Reality. Once in this state, we recognize that pain is simply a necessary part of living. And as we navigate pain with equanimity, we begin to open ourselves to *experiencing* the goodness, wonder, beauty, and magic of the universe. With this acceptance comes discernment about when to express compassion and when to enforce boundaries. In particular, we note and have compassion for the hurtful, selfish, or narcissistic actions and behaviors of others that tend to draw us away from Authentic Living. And while we remain present to and aware of these painful truths, we also establish boundaries on the level of engagement we choose with others. On the receiving end, we invite our friends and guides to lovingly, yet directly, tell us when we drift into our own hurtful, selfish, or narcissistic actions and behaviors, and then to challenge and encourage us to shift back into Authentic Living.

For example, we can feel sadness over the immaturity of a wayward child, yet refuse to enable dysfunctional or addictive behaviors, even when that child rejects us. We can practice a meditative martial art (yoga, Tai Chi, or Qi Gong) and share vulnerably in our small groups, yet end relationships that compromise our values or tax our sanity.

So, while Authentic Living is a state of peace, serenity, gratitude, and vulnerability, it is also a place of strength, purpose, direction, and, surprisingly, *empowerment*.

As a fluid state rather than a fixed destination, entrance into Authentic Living by no means implies perpetual nirvana. The borders to Delusion, Comfort, and Suffering are always beckoning, and we can easily drift into these states, or plunge even lower into Escape, Isolation, or Numbness. Remaining present and awake requires living with the vexing mysteries of the universe, where the only absolutes are Love, Pain, and change. Staying in this northeast state requires a lifetime commitment to awareness practices, including candor, gratitude, curiosity, compassion, and courage, and the others listed in the table on page 17.

Referring back to the full-body CT scan analogy, even with regular stress tests and nutritional supplements, you may still suffer a stroke or heart attack. However, daily well-care practices (good diet, regular exercise, low-stress living) significantly improve your chances of living a long and active life.

Conscious Awareness (or simply, Consciousness) means paying attention to what's really going on at any moment—in our relationship with ourselves as well as in our interactions with others and the world. People in other States of Being (Comfort, Escape, Delusion, Suffering, or Numbness) may seek to draw us out of Authentic Living. Our two bywords must remain *compassion* and *boundaries*. Our mantra or self-talk must be "I see you. I respect you. I care for you. And I choose not to connect with you at an unconscious or hurtful level. I choose to distance myself from relationships that involve complaining, concealing, entitlement, control, or other behaviors that sabotage Authenticity."

———

Knowing the vigilance required, if you choose to stay in Authentic Living, consider that you will need to interweave three basic practices into your life: **Solitude**, **Community**, and **Service**. Solitude means distancing yourself from the din and distractions of the world and simply experiencing both your own company and the quiet, ever-present wonders of Reality. Solitude opens space for personal reflection. It enables you to take stock of your relationships, sense of life purpose, identity, and beliefs.

I encourage you to find your own nurturing mix of solitude practices, including silence, prayer, meditation, study, journaling, martial arts, and forbearance (the intentional denial of anything that distracts you from Reality). Solitude also implies disciplines, such as specific and regular physical fitness regimens and a healthy diet, as ways to heighten and sustain alertness. In essence, solitude disciplines are all forms of personal cleansing: taking stock of your possessions, and purifying mind, body, and spirit.

You found and worked with guides who helped you navigate into Authentic Living. To stay in this state, commit to retaining a supportive Community, a "personal board of directors" or a cabinet of counselors and aware friends who encourage you when you falter and challenge you when you drift into resistance or denial.

Loving friends will also point out your blind spots and any habits that sabotage you and your relationships. The best leaders have a mentor; the best coaches have their own coach; superior athletes train with a team.

As with seeking a guide or mentor, the onus is on you to form your advisory cabinet. Perhaps start with one like-minded, awareness-seeking person. Put out the intention for others to come into your life. Develop a vision statement for your new group and set some simple ground rules. Work at it. Seek diversity. Be open to including people who may at first "push your buttons." Often, they are the ones who have the greatest gift for you.

Vibrant communities regularly take time to appreciate one another. They celebrate breakthroughs, laugh at their foibles, and bless one another for simply *being*. Community members use the unexpected, no-reason-in-particular I-love-you personal note, phone call, or email to encourage one another. And when you feel down or lost, they're the people "who know the song in your heart and can sing it back to you when you've forgotten the words."[12] Commit to having these people in your life—and hold them dear.

The final discipline for sustained Authentic Living is the spirit of Service: giving of yourself to uplift others or serve the world. One of the highest manifestations of love is the spontaneous and unmeasured expression of your gifts in service to others. In Authentic Living, your life *becomes* an act of service, without conscious thought. Recalling the conduit analogy, you simply show up as your True Self and let Love flow through you. In the Comfort state, your life is about you. In Authentic Living, you are about life.

Service also means putting your whole self into your efforts, with discipline (doing your homework and honoring your agreements) and confidence, without whining or second-guessing. You commit to doing your best with or without inspiration, reciprocity, or recognition, inside or outside your comfort zone, in the day-in, day-out toil of living, *for as long as it takes*. While you may be tempted to recede into the martyrdom of Suffering, this is less likely if you choose to serve out of love, and if you have a supportive community watching for drifts back into sabotaging behaviors.

As service becomes instinctive, you'll find increas-

Acts of Kindness

- Actively listen to another person's story without offering advice.
- Check in on someone who is struggling.
- Show active interest in another person's work or hobbies.
- Cheerfully clean the kitchen.
- Let your kids teach you something.
- Offer genuine and specific appreciation toward others. Catch them doing something good.
- Do something you love and invite someone you care about to experience it with you.

Remember: It's not the act itself; it's the spirit (or attitude) you *bring* to the act.

ing fulfillment in the generous expression of your wholeness, rather than in superficial rewards. You will derive deep satisfaction from being with, helping, or simply *seeing* others (and need no recognition for having done so). Over time, service can become more a mind-set than a measurable act, as natural as breathing. And as you serve out of your True Self, you launch an upward spiral of authenticity that inspires others to express their True Selves.

Acts of service don't have to be big. Measurement and comparison are irrelevant. Often, the most memorable forms of service are simple, random acts of kindness, where your actions say to another person, "You are special. I care about you." The **Acts of Kindness** table on the previous page offers some everyday suggestions.

Drifting into Other States and How to Recover

Go easy on yourself. This isn't a contest to be the "most aware person" in your circle of relationships. Remember, Authentic Living is a marathon, not a sprint. It's about equanimity, not competition. As described earlier, the boundaries between Authentic Living and the adjacent states are unguarded and tempting, and it's easy to drift back into old patterns. Further, when your solitude disciplines grow monotonous, your support community seems absent, and service feels like drudgery, the adjacent states may lure you back into comfortable, delusional, or numbing orbits. Here's how this can happen.

Comparison, measurement, and competition, the hallmarks of Comfort, create a duality (me versus them) and often trigger a drift away from Authentic Living. It's easy to fall for the allure of the security-conscious, material world, unconsciously drifting from appreciation back to entitlement, or from equanimity back to power. Alternatively, you might drift south into the loveless pain of resentment over the indiscretions or betrayals of others, or the shame around your own failings. Even while practicing Solitude, Community, and Service disciplines, you'll occasionally feel like the love isn't there. You'll slip into a funk or depression, and old shadows (resentment, anxiety, or unworthiness) will sneak out at the least opportune moment to derail your awareness.

These drifts certainly occur for me. Every summer, after our traditional holiday with our children, I'll fall into a modest depression, contemplating my advancing years, missed opportunities, or fragmented life plan. I have a good old time beating myself up. A decade ago, I would either ruminate in anxiety for a couple of weeks or immerse myself in distractions to mask my self-induced stress. Now, I simply accept the depression. At first it's unpleasant and often emotional—a blend of anxiety,

Drifts from Authentic Living

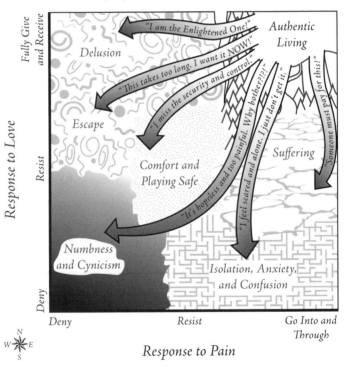

sadness, and shame—and I'm tempted to distract myself with activities. But I stay in it. Eventually—and much sooner than when I resisted—it passes. I then choose to fill the void left by the depression with gratitude: for my family, my mind, my vocational opportunities, my circle of advisors and friends, my health, and so forth. These depressions are now much less frequent, their duration shorter, and their pain less intense. So, as a general rule, when you feel anxious, depressed, or just down, and you can't seem to get out of it, get *into* it. Trust that it will pass.

When your disciplines are strong and your life is going very well, a more subtle, yet devious, drift may occur. You may wave a banner of self-righteous aware-ness. You may feel "enlightened," as though you have "transcended" the suffering that others must endure: "Gee, I feel sorry for those unaware pilgrims who have not dealt with their baggage, faced their demons, and released their past—like I have. I feel this blissful, on-going communion with the universe. I wish everyone could have what I've achieved." This is just another form of narcissism. As shown in the **Delusion and Reality** figure, *any* attempt to increase Love while denying or resisting Pain is delusional.

A proven way to shorten drift time is simply continuous monitoring. Commit to being an interested but detached observer of your own life, celebrating the joys, experiencing the trials, and regularly scanning for drifts.

Delusion and Reality

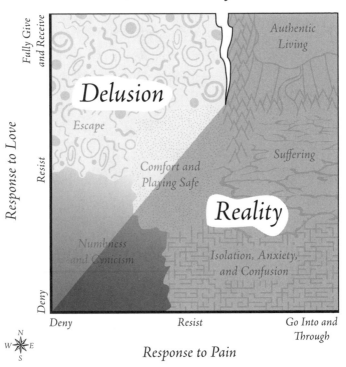

Enlist your personal advisory board to tell you when they see you drifting. Acknowledge and take responsibility for your drifts: "Okay [sigh], it looks like I've done it again." Breathe, relax, and even *laugh* about your own frailty and failings. Then forgive yourself. Forgive those who have let you down. After the forgiveness, *let it go*. That was then, this is now. Reexamine and if necessary reset your boundaries. Communicate and enforce them. Choose (yet again) to be in relationships that bring vibrancy to your life. Develop the courage to end relationships that drain you. Acknowledge, forgive, and recommit. Remember, this journey lasts a lifetime. It's your life. You are worth it.

Clearly, drifts will happen. You can't avoid them. You can, however, notice them, acknowledge and experience them, and then shift back to Authentic Living. At these times, rather than obsessing about your drift into the adjacent states, simply own it, experience it, and release it. But no matter what the form or duration of your drift, you can practice your solitude disciplines and enlist your personal advisory board to help you shift back to the northeast as quickly as you drifted.

To accelerate your return to Authentic Living, consider *loving* your frailties and failings. Embrace failings as part of your Reality, the in-the-moment truth about you. As you own your failings, consider the hidden gift they might have for you. As you examine your shortcomings, taking responsibility for them without letting them dominate or smother you, invite their transformation into something positive. For example, consider shifting your nagging inner critic, perfectionist, or workaholic into an inner encourager. Transform your bottled rage (toward a selfish business partner or inconsiderate relative) into an internal sentry that helps you set and enforce your boundaries with cynics, addicts, narcissists, and others who threaten your awareness. Shift the focus of your Risk Manager's wisdom from playing defense and looking for downsides into a perpetual curiosity and wonder for life, asking, "What can I learn from this moment or from this experience?"

The more you can accept, even embrace, the mystery and paradox of Authentic Living, the more clarity, peace, and freedom will emerge, naturally, in your life. Trust that in all the apparent chaos, Authentic Living is a place of goodness and order. In fact, Authentic Living is transcendent—that is, beyond what we can conceive.

You Have the Map—
Now Plot Your Journey

Look again at the Love↔Pain map. Identify your current "home state" and the orbits in which you tend to spin. Take responsibility for your current location and default orbits. Cast off the words of the victim. No one is "making" you stay anywhere you do not wish to be. In addition, take a fearless moral inventory of yourself, celebrating the causes for gratitude in your life, and owning any and all areas where you are out of integrity with yourself or others. When you screw up (and you will), clean up your own messes.

Concurrently, begin to assemble your personal advisory board and small group. At a minimum, enlist one strong friend or guide who will advise you, encourage you, and challenge you on your journey. Open yourself to the possibility that new allies may appear in your life in unlikely places (your eccentric uncle who doesn't say much, but has been a devoted mentor to the teen next door; or your flakey artist friend, whose house is a perpetual mess, but whose face holds a perpetual smile). Choose personal board members who have depth and maturity in the areas where you seek improvement.

The Whole Map with Various Orbits

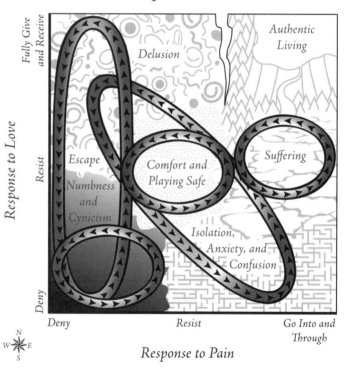

Enlist confidants who will challenge your rationalizations, excuses, and defenses.

Be open to possibility. Consider that *anyone* who crosses your path is a candidate friend, advisor, or guide. With this mind-set, trust that the *exactly right* people will enter your life. When the student is ready, the teacher(s) will appear.

Finally, view Authentic Living as a means and not an end. See this state as a platform for experiencing and sharing in realities that transcend what our restricted minds can grasp. This may sound a little woo-woo and New Age if you're spinning in comfortable, delusional, or suffering orbits. It's easy to be dismissive or cynical, especially when all you're after is some pain relief or a little more love.

But if you are willing to release the constraining beliefs bred in Comfort (remember the trapeze bar), Authentic Living offers a springboard for much more expansive views of, well, *everything*. And if you've been living your life in a fog, Authentic Living offers you a base camp above the clouds to ponder transcendent realities. Like a seasoned Sherpa living in the clear air of an alpine plateau, once you've committed your life to Authentic Living, the eternal sky of transcendent awareness beckons.

A closing insight: Many of us living in Western culture are driven to be the best and the fastest in all pursuits. We apply to our Awareness Journey the same competitive energies that drove our worldly success or relationship conquests. If you are hardwired for action, constantly striving, thrashing, pushing, or emoting, try a new approach. On the path to Authentic Living, fall silent, breathe deeply, and appreciate that Authentic Living is simply *being* on the path. You are *already there*.

In the silence, simply receive the love that has been and will always be your birthright.

Appendixes

Appendix A: Whole-Life Audit

Using the chart on the following page, consider the areas of your life identified in the first column. For each area, come up with a word or phrase that describes your relationship to that area. Examples {. . .} are provided for most areas. Write the word or phrase in the middle column. Then look deeply within yourself: Is your relationship with the area really working for you? Are you pleased, happy, content, or at ease with your relationship to the area? This is a "yes/no" question. "Sometimes," "maybe," or "sort of" all mean "no." If you have a heartfelt "yes," then circle YES for that area, and be grateful that this area of your life is working well for you. Otherwise, circle NO, and answer the following questions:

- What do you want to happen?
- What steps are you prepared to take to change your relationship to the area?

Whole-Life Audit

Area of Your Life	Use a Word or Phrase to Describe Your Relationship to the Area	Is It Working for You? <u>YES</u> or <u>NO</u> (Circle One)	
Time	{Never Enough, Frantic, Ample}	YES	NO
Your Vocation	{Robot, Passion, Sandbox, Prison, Sport}	YES	NO
Money	{Obsession, Privilege, Gateway, Tool}	YES	NO
Your Marriage or Lover Relationship	{Battle, Soul Mate, Synergy, Joyful}	YES	NO
Your Children	{Joy, Distant, Entitlement, Playful}	YES	NO
Your Extended Family	{Tolerance, Loving, Acrimony}	YES	NO
Other Relationship: _____		YES	NO
Your Body	{Temple, Out of Control, Shame, Respect}	YES	NO
A Higher Power; Spirituality	{Surrender, Curiosity, Ambivalence, Awe}	YES	NO
Your Sense of Life Purpose	{Unknown, Clear, Scattered, Unfulfilled}	YES	NO
Your Approach to Life Today	{Intense, Conscious, Reactive}	YES	NO
Your Self	{Loving, Critical, Trusting}	YES	NO
"Wild Card" Category _____		YES	NO

Appendix B: Whole-Life Relationship Audit

Using the chart on the following page, consider the key relationships in your life (identified in the first column). In each relationship, consider the level of Authenticity you experience, ranging from Blaming, Complaining, Hurtful to Transparent, Synergistic, Caring. Each of the five interaction levels has three divisions, representing the low, mid, and high end of the respective level. Place an "X" in the box to the right of each category that best describes your interactions within the relationship. Then look deeply within yourself: For each relationship, is the level of Authenticity really working for you? Are you pleased, happy, content, or at ease with this relationship? If so, be grateful that this relationship is working well for you. If not, answer the following questions:

- What do you want to have happen in the relationship?
- What difficult conversation have you been avoiding?

- What steps are you prepared to take to shift the relationship to a higher Authenticity level?

General Approach to Interactions					
	Blaming, Complaining, Hurtful	Controlled, Manage the Relationship	Polite, Passive, Nice	Open, Collaborative, Appreciative	Transparent, Synergistic, Caring
Relationship Category					
Spouse					
Children					
Extended Family					
Peers at Work					
Subordinates at Work					
Superiors at Work					
Friends					
Small Group					
The World / Society					
Higher Power					
Yourself					
Other: _____					

Appendix C: Example Small Group Covenant

Vision for Our Group

We are a caring group of committed peers and friends, meeting on a regular basis for safe, unforced sharing of our lives. We maintain an environment of mutual trust, integrity, and tenderness, where participants are truthful with one another, offering and receiving counsel, holding one another accountable, and pointing out blind spots. Our time together is a blend of learning, sharing, discussing, experiencing, and challenging. We share adventures, celebrations, and pure fun. More specifically:

- We explore vocational stories, challenges, issues, dilemmas, problems, blind spots, and celebrations.
- We explore personal stories, challenges, issues, dilemmas, problems, blind spots, and celebrations.
- We explore family and interpersonal stories, challenges, issues, dilemmas, problems, blind spots, and celebrations.
- We socialize with one another. We enjoy one another's company.

- We meet at a comfortable, consistent, and safe location.
- We meet once a month for four hours.
- We go off together for a retreat once a year.

A Group Member's Code of Conduct

- I will respect confidentiality.
- I will be present in the moment.
- I will stay around when times get tough.
- I will be on time and stay until the end.
- I will speak my truth.
- I will ask for what I want.
- I will take care of myself.
- I am willing to make mistakes.
- I am willing to laugh at myself.
- I will own my feelings.
- I will own my judgments.
- I will honor others, without blaming or shaming.
- I will ask permission before offering advice.

Appendix D: Guidelines on How to End a Relationship

You're in a difficult, energy-draining relationship. You've examined the relationship from multiple perspectives, looking for any possible way to salvage some form of meaningful contact. And you've concluded that either the other person is incapable of an authentic relationship or the effort to save the relationship simply isn't worth it. You now wish to end the relationship.

You can do so in one of two ways. One option is to become "invisible." With this "Teflon" approach, you continue to have cordial, transactional exchanges with the person as necessary (e.g., encounters at work or in other public settings), but you avoid all other contact. You don't return phone calls or emails except for purely transactional purposes. No proactive communication. When the other person makes overtures for additional contact, you either make an excuse or politely decline. In many cases, the relationship will die out on its own.

The second approach is to have a direct encounter with the person. This may occur when you are confronted by the person about the state of the relationship, or you may feel out of integrity with yourself when using the avoidance approach and therefore seek honest closure. Here are some guidelines for ending the relationship cleanly:

1. **Prepare for the encounter.** Develop a mind-set of compassion for the other person, irrespective of any discomfort, disdain, or even loathing you may feel toward them. When you can view them with compassion, the emotions that inevitably arise in these difficult encounters will have less impact on you. Complement the compassion with a sense of resolve and commitment that you are intentionally ending the relationship. No equivocation, no negotiation. You've made the decision; it's over. Compassion and resolve form the strong platform for having the conversation.

   Set aside judgments of the other person and assume they will enter the conversation maturely, openly, and cleanly. Nevertheless, be prepared for an emotional, immature response from them. In other words, hope for the best and plan for the worst.

   If you feel your own emotions rising from previous exchanges with the other person, share these feelings with a third party, ideally someone who is uninvolved with the relationship dynamic. When you can release your own fear, anger, embarrassment, or sadness before the actual encounter, these emotions are less likely to sabotage you during the encounter.

Whenever possible, schedule the encounter at a time when you are prepared and rested, and can be present for the other person. Also, choose a neutral venue, where you have the opportunity to walk away if the conversation turns ugly (i.e., not your home, your office, or other location where you might be "cornered").

2. **Launch the conversation.** Clearly state that the closure is your choice. Speak using "inarguable truths": a blend of irrefutable facts, your feelings, and your own judgments about the relationship or the other person, and your specific wants for yourself. Make it clear that your decision is all about you, not the other person. Avoid blaming the other person for anything and resist the temptation to rationalize your decision. Blame and rationalization invite argument, further churning the emotions and prolonging the process.

As an example, consider the following statements:

"John, for the past few weeks [months, years], I have found myself avoiding contact with you. I have not returned your phone calls or emails."

"I've felt uncomfortable [uneasy, anxious] around you."

"When you made crude remarks in front of my daughter [mocked your brother to the point of tears at the party last

Friday or any other verifiable behavior], I felt embarrassed [angry, scared].”

“I choose to be in relationships where I can feel relaxed, safe, and open. Sadly, I've concluded this is not possible in our relationship. And so, while we may have occasional inter- actions [as required by the job, at family events, in public settings], I've chosen to end our relationship [I wish to limit our interactions to work-only topics].”

3. **Anticipate an emotional response.** This is where your platform of compassion and resolve is most important. Never negotiate with or try to rationalize emotions. Your role here is simply to listen and reflect back until either the other person's emotion is dissipated or the time seems right to move to closure. For example:

John: “I can't believe you'd make those accusations about me. I thought you were one of my best friends. You're not so 'pure' yourself, pal. How about the time you . . .”

You: “I get that you sense I'm making accusations and that you thought we were best friends. And you feel there have also been times when I haven't been so pure myself. I can understand that.”

John: “Yeah, and our spouses are best friends. You care nothing about the investment my wife and I have made in this relationship. You're just a selfish jerk.”

You: "I see that you sense I don't care about the friendship our wives share and the investment you and Frances have made in our relationship. And you think I'm being selfish."

Continue listening and reflecting until the other person's emotions start to wane. You might then move to closure by validating (yet not agreeing with) his viewpoint, and then asking the key question:

You: "John, thank you for sharing how you see it. As I put myself in your shoes, I can see how you would feel that way. Is there anything more you'd like to share?"

This last question is crucial. If the person has more to say, repeat the listen-reflect loop and continue asking, with compassion, the "Is there more?" question until the person is complete.

4. **Closure.** Definitively conclude the conversation and the relationship:

   "John, I'm glad we have had this exchange [discussion, conversation]. I wish you the best. Goodbye."

   And leave.

5. **What to do if the other person becomes volatile or abusive, or you find your own compassion-resolve platform beginning to buckle.** Whenever you are losing your own sense of presence and maturity in a conversation, end the conversation immediately. You might say something like:

   "I notice that I'm beginning to lose my own composure here.

Perhaps we can continue this discussion at another time, but for now, I'm choosing to leave."

And leave.

6. **Leaving the door open.** Ending a relationship need not be forever. Depending on the receptivity and maturity of the other person at the time of the encounter and on your own openness to a new relationship with the person, you may express your willingness to consider a new relationship at a later date. For example:

"My decision to end [limit] our interactions is for the present time. In a few months [years], I may be willing to consider a new relationship between us. But for now, I need some space."

Be aware that this approach may trigger a dialogue around timing and conditions for the "new relationship." Either have this well thought out prior to the conversation, or defer it to a time when you are fully prepared to consider the new relationship.

If you have a hard time articulating clearly when under stress, practice the closing conversation with a trusted confidant or by talking to yourself in a mirror. This will help you refine your position and strengthen your resolve. It will also help you be more concise during the actual conversation.

Guidelines on How to End a Relationship

Typically, the longer you have delayed ending a relationship, the more difficult and painful the closing encounter. Taking the steps outlined here can help make the process more bearable for both parties. Commit to building a platform of compassion and resolve. Release your own emotions so you can go into the encounter as cleanly as possible. State your inarguable truths about your view of the relationship and your decision to end it. Listen and reflect back whatever the other person expresses. When the other person is complete, definitively end the relationship.

In most instances you'll wonder why you waited so long.

Appendix E: The Annotated Love↔Pain Map

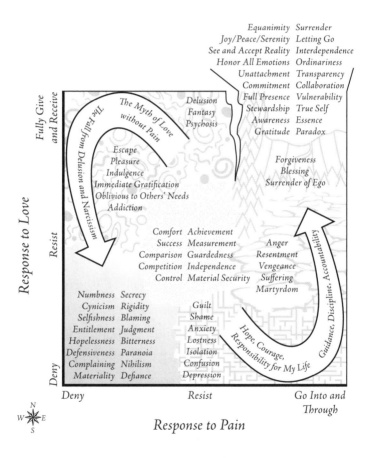

Equanimity Surrender
Joy/Peace/Serenity Letting Go
See and Accept Reality Interdependence
Honor All Emotions Ordinariness
Unattachment Transparency
Commitment Collaboration
Full Presence Vulnerability
Stewardship True Self
Awareness Essence
Gratitude Paradox

Delusion
Fantasy
Psychosis

The Myth of Love without Pain

The Fall from Delusion and Narcissism

Escape
Pleasure
Indulgence
Immediate Gratification
Oblivious to Others' Needs
Addiction

Forgiveness
Blessing
Surrender of Ego

Fully Give and Receive

Response to Love

Resist

Comfort Achievement
Success Measurement
Comparison Guardedness
Competition Independence
Control Material Security

Anger
Resentment
Vengeance
Suffering
Martyrdom

Guidance, Discipline, Accountability

Numbness Secrecy
Cynicism Rigidity
Selfishness Blaming
Entitlement Judgment
Hopelessness Bitterness
Defensiveness Paranoia
Complaining Nihilism
Materiality Defiance

Guilt
Shame
Anxiety
Lostness
Isolation
Confusion
Depression

Hope, Courage, Responsibility for My Life

Deny

Deny

Resist

Go Into and Through

Response to Pain

N
W ✳ E
S

Appendix F: Bibliography

The following resources (books, audio, and workshops) can help guide us toward Authentic Living and greater personal awareness.

Bob Buford's wonderful series on transition—*Half Time, Game Plan, Stuck in Half Time,* and *Finishing Well*—provides many tips and tools for changing your life plan from success to significance. For more information go to www.bobbuford.com.

Anthony de Mello has been celebrated as one of the most important inspirational and contemplative writers of our time. His books offer stories and parables from a variety of traditions, both ancient and modern. His book *Wellsprings* is a collection of teachings and spiritual exercises that blend the ancient traditions of the East with the psychological and philosophical perspectives of the West. Other de Mello classics include *Awareness* and *Song of the Bird*. For more information go to www.demello.org.

Gay and Kathlyn Hendricks lead an International Learning Center that teaches core skills for conscious living. Their groundbreaking work over the past three decades has guided people to more creativity, love, and vitality, through the power of conscious relationships and whole-person learning. For more information go to www.hendricks.com.

The **Hoffman Process** is a one-week residential course for adults seeking deep personal transformation. Based on independently published university research, the Hoffman Process provides more and longer-lasting benefits than any other program. In its forty-one-year history, thousands of people in leadership positions have found this to be the perfect place for doing their most personal inner work, resulting in a life of authenticity, success, creativity, and joy. For more information go to www.hoffmaninstitute.org.

Don Riso and Russ Hudson are two of the foremost teachers on awareness and presence. Their work centers on the Enneagram personality typing system. Their signature book, *The Wisdom of the Enneagram*, provides a comprehensive, easy-to-understand explanation of this profound model of psychology and spirituality. For more information go to www.enneagraminstitute.com.

Byron Katie is a noted author and guide whose books and programs teach people how to end their own suffering and wake up to reality. As she leads people through the powerful process of inquiry called *The Work*, they find that their stressful beliefs—about life, other people, or themselves—radically shift and their lives are changed forever. For more information go to www.thework.com.

Jack Kornfield is one of the leading spiritual teachers in America. His approach emphasizes compassion, loving kindness, and the profound path of mindful presence, all offered in simple, accessible ways in his books, CDs, classes, and retreats. *After the Ecstasy, the Laundry* draws on the experiences and insights of leaders and practitioners within the Buddhist, Christian, Jewish, Hindu, and Sufi traditions. The book offers a uniquely intimate and honest understanding of how the modern spiritual journey unfolds—and how we can prepare our hearts for awakening. For more information go to www.jackkornfield.org.

Gerald May practiced medicine and psychiatry for twenty-five years before becoming a senior fellow in contemplative theology and psychology at the **Shalem**

Institute for Spiritual Formation in Bethesda, Maryland. His many books blend spirituality and psychology, and include *Addiction and Grace, Care of Mind/ Care of Spirit, Will and Spirit,* and *The Dark Night of the Soul.* For more information go to www.shalem.org.

Thomas Merton is widely acclaimed as one of the most influential American spiritual writers of the past century. Thousands of readers have drawn strength from his words as well as the witness of his life, which was essentially the living out of a contemplative vision. His autobiography, *The Seven Storey Mountain*, appears on lists of the one hundred most important books of the century. *New Seeds of Contemplation* is a contemplation classic that reawakens the dormant inner depths of the spirit so long neglected by Western man. For more information go to www.mertoninstitute.org.

Henri Nouwen was a Dutch Catholic priest and writer who authored forty books on the spiritual life. Father Nouwen spent his life helping people respond to the universal "yearning for love, unity, and communion that doesn't go away." *The Wounded Healer* and *Return of the Prodigal Son* are two of his many books on

awareness and forgiveness. For more information go to
www.henrinouwen.org.

Dave Phillips is a speaker, mentor, stunt man, professional athlete, world-record holder, and business owner—all in his spare time. He has become the Young Presidents' Organization "Life Purpose Guy," leading CEOs through his proven process for digging down to the most important parts of life, and then living these with integrity. His book, *The Three Big Questions*, offers a step-by-step process for uncovering your life purpose, mission, and vision. For more information go to www.dphillips.com.

Richard Rohr is a Franciscan priest and founder of the **Center for Action and Contemplation** in Albuquerque, New Mexico. A prolific writer and speaker, Father Rohr integrates multiple themes into his communications, including the integration of action and contemplation, community building, peace and justice issues, male spirituality, the Enneagram, and eco-spirituality. Some of his best-known books include *Everything Belongs* and *Radical Grace*. For more information go to www.cacradicalgrace.org.

Bibliography

Eckhart Tolle's profound yet simple teachings have helped millions of people throughout the world find inner peace and greater fulfillment in their lives. At the core of his teachings lies the transformation of consciousness, a spiritual awakening that he sees as the next step in human evolution. In addition to his two best sellers, *The Power of Now* and *A New Earth*, Eckhart has written a book designed for meditative reading entitled *Stillness Speaks*. For more information go to www. eckharttolle.com.

Ken Wilber has been dubbed one of the greatest philosophers of the past century and arguably the greatest theoretical psychologist of all time. He writes on psychology, philosophy, mysticism, ecology, and spiritual evolution. His work formulates what he calls an "integral theory of consciousness." I recommend his more recent books: *The Integral Vision* and *Integral Life Practice: A 21st-Century Blueprint for Physical Health, Emotional Balance, Mental Clarity, and Spiritual Awakening*. Also consider his audio series: *Kosmic Consciousness* and *A Brief History of Everything*. For more information go to www.kenwilber.com.

Bibliography

Robert White is a frequent keynote speaker and workshop leader on organizational leadership, successfully handling rapid change, entrepreneurial success, and being more personally effective. His book, *Living an Extraordinary Life,* outlines the imperative of taking personal responsibility for our lives. For more information go to www.extraordinarybook.com.

Notes

1. M. Scott Peck, *The Road Less Traveled* (New York: Simon & Schuster, 1987).

2. Byron Katie is a noted author and guide whose books and programs teach people how to end their own suffering and wake up to reality. As she leads people through the powerful process of inquiry called *The Work*, they find that their stressful beliefs—about life, other people, or themselves—radically shift and their lives are changed forever. For more information go to www.thework.com.

3. The "Risk Manager" is a term originally conceived by Cliff Barry of Shadow Work® Seminars. Cliff and his associates help individuals harness the power of their shadows through seminars, facilitator trainings, and individual coaching sessions. They may be reached via email at shadowwk@frii.com, or via their web site, www.shadowwork.com.

4. *Alcoholics Anonymous* (Hazelden Information Press, 1986) and *Twelve Steps and Twelve Traditions/B-2* (1996).

5. Outward Bound is a nonprofit educational organization that serves people of all ages and backgrounds through active learning expeditions that inspire character development, self-discovery, and service both in and out of the classroom. For more information go to www.outwardbound.org.

Notes

6. Step Four of the Twelve-Step Program invites us to make a searching and fearless moral inventory of ourselves. Where are we out of integrity with ourselves or others?

7. Step Nine of the Twelve-Step Program: To make direct amends to all persons whom you have harmed wherever possible, except when to do so would injure them or others.

8. I heard this potent, unaccredited quote on resentment at one of my retreats. I welcome feedback from readers, so I can credit the source in the next release.

9. John Heider, *The Tao of Leadership* (New York: Bantam, 1996).

10. Danaan Perry, "Parable of the Trapeze," *Warriors of the Heart* (Seattle, WA: Earth Stewards Network, 1990).

11. Rumi is the shorthand name for the thirteenth century Persian mystic who is now one of the most widely read poets in the world. Although Rumi's works were written in Persian, his importance transcends national and ethnic borders. For more information go to www.rumi.net.

12. I heard this lovely, unaccredited quote on friendship at another one of my retreats. I welcome feedback from readers, so I can credit the source in the next release.

About the Author

Jim Warner is an entrepreneur and life-transition expert with insights grounded in a rare combination of experience and empathy. From 1980 through 1992, he skillfully navigated the peaks and valleys of the burgeoning software industry. First, he led his own firm from startup through phenomenal growth. Midstage, he forged beyond downsizing to successful resurgence. Ultimately, Warner sold his company, with visions of comfortable, secure, and satisfying days ahead. But the transition was far rockier than he expected.

In his midforties Jim entered a three-year period of introspection and questioning: How to rejuvenate relationships with his family and friends? How to leverage his existing and latent skills and interests in a meaningful way? How to overcome personal weaknesses that blocked his fulfillment?

OnCourse International is the product of Jim's taking stock and heightened awareness. Today, he is a dedicated coach, advisor, and facilitator to senior executives, guiding them into candid, creative, and collaborative interactions for enhanced performance, at both the enterprise and whole-life levels. Having worked with more than 2,000 CEOs, executive teams from fast-growth, high-performance companies, and dozens of couples navigating difficult midlife transitions, Jim is a recognized expert at helping individuals, couples, and teams achieve greater self-awareness, authentic and productive communication, more fulfilling relationships—and more satisfying lives.

Jim is the author of *Aspirations of Greatness: Mapping the Midlife Leader's Reconnection to Self and Soul* as well as the audio series *When Having It All Isn't Enough*. Whether for entire corporations, executive teams, small groups, couples, or individuals, Jim is an expert in breeding clean, productive interactions and eliminating destructive and draining behavioral ruts. He is also a sought-after speaker at industry conferences and corporate events.

Jim has been married thirty-two years and enjoys enriching relationships with his three adult children. He is a graduate of the University of Michigan as well as an alumnus of Harvard Business School (OPM program). He is a member of the World Presidents' Organization. For more information go to www.oncoursein.com.